Social Stories Book

UNIVERSITY OF
BIRMINGHAM

KT-558-579

2009

of related interest

Asperger's Syndrome
A Guide for Parents and Professionals
Tony Attwood
Foreword by Lorna Wing
ISBN 1 85302 577 1

Playing, Laughing and Learning with Children on the Autism Spectrum
A Practical Resource of Play Ideas for Parents and Carers
Julia Moor
ISBN 1 84310 060 6

Relationship Development Intervention with Young Children
Social and Emotional Development Activities for Asperger
Syndrome, Autism, PDD and NLD
Steven E. Gutstein and Rachelle K. Sheely
ISBN 1 84310 714 7

Relationship Development Intervention with Children, Adolescents and Adults
Social and Emotional Development Activities for Asperger
Syndrome, Autism, PDD and NLD
Steven E. Gutstein and Rachelle K. Sheely
ISBN 1 84310 717 1

Available in a two volume set ISBN 84310 720 1

Giggle Time – Establishing the Social Connection
A Program to Develop the Communication Skills of Children with Autism
Susan Aud Sonders
ISBN 1 84310 716 3

My Social Stories Book

Carol Gray
and Abbie Leigh White

Illustrated by Sean McAndrew

Jessica Kingsley Publishers
London and New York

All rights reserved. No part of this publication may be reproduced in any material form (including photocopying or storing it in any medium by electronic means and whether or not transiently or incidentally to some other use of this publication) without the written permission of the copyright owner except in accordance with the provisions of the Copyright, Designs and Patents Act 1988 or under the terms of a licence issued by the Copyright Licensing Agency Ltd, 90 Tottenham Court Road, London, England W1P 9HE. Applications for the copyright owner's written permission to reproduce any part of this publication should be addressed to the publisher.

Warning: The doing of an unauthorised act in relation to a copyright work may result in both a civil claim for damages and criminal prosecution.

The right of Carol Gray and Abbie Leigh White to be identified as authors of this work has been asserted by them in accordance with the Copyright, Designs and Patents Act 1988

First published in the United Kingdom in 2002
by Jessica Kingsley Publishers Ltd
116 Pentonville Road
London N1 9JB, England
and
29 West 35th Street, 10th fl.
New York, NY 10001-2299, USA
www.jkp.com

Second impression 2003
Third impression 2003
Fourth impression 2003
Fifth impression 2003

Text copyright © Jenison Public Schools and The Gray Center
for Social Learning and Understanding
Illustrations copyright © Sean McAndrew 2002

Library of Congress Cataloging in Publication Data
Gray, Carol, 1952-
    My social stories book / Carol Gray
      p. cm.
    Summary: Takes autistic children step by step through such activities as using the toilet, brushing their teeth, and wearing a safety belt in the car.
      ISBN 1-85302-950-5 (alk. paper)
      1. Autistic children—Treatment—Juvenile literature. 2. Storytelling—Therapeutic use—Juvenile literature. 3. Autism in children—Treatment—Juvinile literature. 4. Narration (Rhetoric)—Psychological aspects—Juvinle literature. [1. Autism.] I. Title.
RJ506.A9 G697 2001
618.92'898206—dc21

                                                                                2002025682

British Library Cataloguing in Publication Data
A CIP catalogue record for this book is available from the British Library

ISBN 1 85302 950 5

Printed and Bound in Great Britain by
Athenaeum Press, Gateshead, Tyne and Wear

This book is dedicated to the young children
who listen to these stories
and look at the pictures in this book,
and to the parents and professionals
who work on their behalf.

Contents

Chapter Two – Home

Chapter Three – Going Places

Acknowledgements

The editors wish to thank the following individuals for contributing topics for Stories to *My Social Stories Book*

Carolyn Acres of Lubbock, Texas, United States;

Gia Amoree of Westford, Vermont, United States;

Theresa Aunt of Underhill Ctr., Vermont, United States;

Ruth S. Beard of Montpelier, Vermont, United States;

Cathy Bendle of Prince Albert, Saskatchewan, Canada;

Jean Bergman of Burlington, Vermont, United States;

Kathy Blakey of Barre, Vermont, United States;

Beth Burgess of Richford, Vermont, United States;

Christie Cahalan of Waterbury, Vermont, United States;

Marc Carpente of Sudbury, Vermont, United States;

Lisa Castillo of Lubbock, Texas, United States;

Cinda Chaim of St. Albaus, Vermont, United States;

Tina Cleveland of Hardwick, Vermont, United States;

Ruth Cohan of Burlington, Vermont, United States;

Kathleen Cooper of Toronto, Ontario, Canada;

Sandra Culwell of Lubbock, Texas, United States;

Dawn Dowbush of Calgary, Alabama, United States;

Karen Elimelech of Woodbridge, Connecticut, United States;

Linelle Giles of Calgary, Alabama, United States;

Tara Gill of Burlington, Vermont, United States;

Barbie Gore of Lubbock, Texas, United States;

Jo-Anne Gray of Lethbridge, Alabama, United States;

Nancy Hall of East Burke, Vermont, United States;

Barb Hardcastle of Saskatoon, Saskatchewan, Canada;

Beverly Harkema of Hudsonville, Michigan, United States;

Judy Heberle of Woodland, California, United States;

Meredith Horton of Lubbock, Texas, United States;

Libby Hylhouse of Ryegate, Vermont, United States;

Heather Jamison of Sydenham, Ontario, Canada;

Judy Jolin Pickett of Wisconsin, United States;

Greg and Vicky Laewetz Stettler of Alberta, Canada;

Cecil Languerand of Morrisville, Vermont, United States;

Laurie Latornas of Prince Albert, Saskatchewan, Canada;

Julie LeBeau of Colchester, Vermont, United States;

Rita McDonough of Beaconsfield, Quebec, Canada;

Anne Mcintosh of Prince Albert, Saskatchewan, Canada;

Laurie McKee of Lubbock, Texas, United States;

Barbara McKeon of Randolph, Vermont United, States;

Deb MeCake of Chatham, Ontario, Canada;

Dave MeCarthy of Saskatoon, Saskatchewan, Canada;

Rhea Melton of Spur, Texas, United States;

Elizabeth Newman of Hinesburg, Vermont, United States;

Jennifer Ormerod of Fairfax, Vermont, United States;

Leslie Owens of Solon, Ohio, United States;

Lori E. Poludin of Quechee, Vermont, United States;

Kathy Reynolds of Cornwall, Vermont, United States;

Valerie Ringey Cornwall Vermont United States;

Kim Roy of North York, Ontario, Canada;

Angel Rubino of Woodstock, Vermont, United States;

Carol Rudd of Rocky Point, New York, United States;

Susan Rump of Thelford, Vermont, United States;

Nicole Sansom of Winnipeg, Manitoba, Canada;

Pat Savinkoff of Abbotsford, British Colombia, Canada;

Melissa Scanlon of Jeffersonville, Vermont, United States;

Mary Beth Schmit of Lubbock, Texas, United States;

Julie Sturm of Lyndonville, Vermont, United States;

Maureen Sullivan of South Burlington, Vermont, United States;

Betty Tholl of Prince Albert, Saskatchewan, Canada;

Misty Vetter of Hendersonville, Tennessee, United States;

Barbara Weintraub of North Clarendon, Vermont United States;

Becky Willey;

Donna Williamson of Bridgewater, Vermont, United States;

Amy Wood of Waitsfield, Vermont, United States.

A Note to Parents and Professionals

My Social Stories Book is an all-new collection of Social Stories for young children with Autistic Spectrum Disorders (ASD). A Social Story is a process that results in a product. As a process, parents and professionals consider the perspective of the child while describing a situation, skill, or concept in terms of relevant social clues, perspectives, and common responses. Each Social Story is developed according to specific guidelines that are based on the learning characteristics of children with ASD. This results in text and illustrations with defining characteristics, among them an overall patient and reassuring quality.

Social Stories are flexible teachers of young children. They describe what most of us dismiss as obvious, patiently considering the world through the eyes of a child with an ASD. A Social Story can inform, reassure, instruct, console, support, praise, and correct children with ASD *and* those who work on their behalf. In less than a decade, Social Stories have earned their place in homes and classrooms around the world. Considering that the very first Social Stories was written for a young child, it is fitting that a book of Social Stories for young children should arrive to celebrate the tenth anniversary. *My Social Stories Book* represents an instructional strategy that we hope will benefit children with ASD – and those who work on their behalf – for many years to come.

The book is organized into three chapters, *Taking Care of Me*, *Home* and *Going Places*. The stories within each chapter cover topics that are frequently encountered in early childhood. For example, in the chapter, *Taking Care of Me*, the stories describes daily routines, such as toileting, taking medicine, and brushing teeth. Although these may appear to be simple topics, anyone who has taught these skills to a young child can attest to their inherent complexities and unexpected challenges!

My Social Stories Book introduces *Social Story Sets*, a new format specifically developed for young children with ASD. A Social Story Set is a collection of very short Stories related to one topic that share a single illustration. Each Story within a Set describes one small part of a skill or concept. A Social Story opens with an introductory Story that introduces the topic. Many Social Story Sets have a concluding Story that further reinforces how the details described in the Stories "work together." The illustration depicts the relationship between the Stories, providing a picture of their collective "gist."

Social Story Sets respect the attention span and learning style of young children with ASD. Children with ASD take note of small details, and learn best when new concepts and skills are presented one step at a time. The stories follow a child's lead by looking at and considering each of the details in a situation or skill, in an effort to capture and maintain a child's interest. A child has the opportunity to consider all of the parts;

to feel comfortable with the details before learning how they work together.

The "overall picture" is exactly what the authors and editors had in mind as they worked with the illustrator, Mr. Sean McAndrew of Kula, Hawaii. Mr. McAndrew is an artist who has two relatives with Asperger Syndrome and impressive professional credentials that include animation work for Disney Studios. His illustrations depict the coexistence of the collective detail of each set of Stories with a reassuring simplicity.

This is a book for children. It is our hope that it will find its way into toy boxes, bookshelves, bed covers, bathrooms, and playrooms. The following ten suggestions are intended as a guide to help you bring these Stories to life:

1. Carefully review each Social Story Set prior to introducing it to a young child. Determine whether it requires modification in order to address a child's individual needs or add interest.

2. Introduce a Story in a manner consistent with its honest, patient and reassuring quality.

3. When reading a Story to a young child for the first time, consider sitting at the child's side and slightly back with the attention jointly focused on the Story. Do not draw attention to your own facial expressions or gestures; these may be gradually introduced as the story becomes more familiar.

4. Read a Story in a quiet setting with a positive, casual, and comfortable attitude. Avoid sharing a Story while a child is upset, or using a Story as a consequence for misbehavior.

5. A child may listen to a single Story, or two, or three, or the entire set. Most Social Stories for young children are introduced one at a time. An adult may choose to review the first Story in a Set, later returning and reading the first and second Stories, gradually working up to reading an entire Set of Stories to a child. This gives the Stories a predictable and reassuring quality, as well as the excitement of being able to predict "what comes next," prior to the introduction of the next Story in the Set.

6. The frequency with which a Social Story Set, or a single Story, is read to a child is dependent upon many factors. Most important is your judgement; most influential is the child's attention. For some children frequent repetition of a Story will increase attention and interest. Other children will become bored with a Story if it is presented too many times. In addition, the Story topic dictates in part how often a Story is reviewed. For example, a Story describing a daily event, such as toileting, may cause you to reach for it far more frequently than a restaurant Story. The golden rule of thumb is to never force a child to attend to a Social Story, and to find a review schedule that is comfortable for all parties.

7. Mr. McAndrew provides a wonderful start; you play a key role in bringing the Stories to life. Encourage and gradually increase a child's participation as each story is reviewed and his/her understanding of the story improves. Be creative. Below are some examples:

(a) Ask the child to point to the part of each illustration that a Story describes.

(b) Collect objects from your own home that are mentioned in the Stories and keep them in a box that you keep to accompany the book. Select objects as indicated and "act out" the Stories.

(c) A more advanced activity: encourage the child to note ties between the text and *decisions* the illustrator made. (Instead of asking, "Can you find_____ in the picture?" try, "What did Mr McAndrew decide to draw here?" This can make the Story more interesting, as well as laying the groundwork for children who in the future may be illustrating their own Social Stories.)

8. A set of crayons or markers is all that is needed to make *My Social Stories Book* into a coloring book! A word of caution: a child with ASD may interpret color in an illustration literally. For example, upon seeing a red shirt on the mother in the illustration accompanying the Story Set about taking turns, a child may mistakenly believe Mom must always wear a red shirt to help children take turns. Color may be a positive addition for

other children; individualizing the Stories with tailored skin, clothing and environment colors. Color is introduced into *My Social Stories Book* at your discretion.

9.   These are *Social Stories*; to use them in isolation is to miss their real value. Whether used individually or in sets, their meaning may be enhanced with the addition of other creative activities. For example, to reinforce the concepts described in the Social Story Set about visiting a grocery store, you may:

(a)   *Role Play* the Story Set by playing "grocery store" with a play cart and groceries.

(b)   *Generalize* the concepts in the Story Set by giving the child a copy of the illustration to hold as she rides in the cart.

(c)   *Act out* the Story Set by reading each Story in sequence while visiting the store.

(d)   *Create related activities* or routines, especially those that help to further structure the child's role in a given situation.

10.   Adding a Story that describes a related activity from the child's own experience will personalize this book. The ideas are endless; a little creativity and effort can go a long way to clarifying and expanding the meaning of a Social Story Set.

Welcome to *My Social Stories Book*, the first book of Social Story Sets for young children. On behalf of the administration of Jenison Public Schools, and all of the Jenison High School students and staff involved in its development, it is our sincere hope that these pages will entertain and inform. Throughout our efforts, the faces and personalities that comprise this unique young audience were in our minds and hearts. Our best wishes to the young children who listen to the Stories and look at the pictures in this book, and to the wonderful parents and professionals who work on their behalf.

Chapter 1

Taking Care of Me

What do I do when I need to use the toilet?

Sometimes I have to go to the toilet. If I have to use a toilet I have two choices:

Tell Mom, Dad, or an adult who can help me.

Go and use the toilet myself.

Using my two choices will help keep my clothes dry.

Where are the toilets?

In my home we have ___ toilets. The toilets are in the bathroom(s).

There is a bathroom

_____.

There is a bathroom

_____.

There is a bathroom

_____.

This is where the bathroom(s) is in my home. If one bathroom is being used, I may have a choice. I may go to another bathroom. I may wait for my turn to use the bathroom.

How do I help others find the toilet in my home?

Sometimes people visit my home. They may need to use a toilet. They know where the bathroom is at their home. They may need to learn where the bathroom is in my home. They may say, "May I use your bathroom?" I can help them by showing them where the bathroom is in my home.

Where are other toilets?

Sometimes people leave their homes to go to other places. If they need a toilet, there is usually one nearby. Each home has a toilet. Stores have toilets. Restaurants have toilets. Museums and amusement parks have toilets. Sometimes I have to go to a toilet when I am not at home. People who are with me can help me find a toilet. I can try to say, "Can you help me find a toilet?"

Time to Wash My Hands

Sometimes my hands get dirty. I may use water and soap to get my hands clean. This is called washing my hands.

Why do I wash my hands?

Washing my hands makes them clean again. Washing my hands helps to keep me healthy. Washing my hands is an intelligent idea. Washing my hands is a healthy thing to do.

When do people wash their hands?

People wash their hands when their hands are dirty. People also wash their hands before they eat and after they haved used the toilet.

An adult knows when I need to wash my hands. Sometimes, I might wash my hands after I have played outside. I may need to wash my hands at another time. I will try to wash my hands when an adult tells me.

How do children learn to wash their hands?

Adults teach children to wash their hands. I am learning to wash my hands. I will use soap and water. These are the steps:

Step 1: Turn on the water.

Step 2: Put soap
on my hands.

Step 3: Rub my hands
together and maybe
add a little water. This
makes soap bubbles.

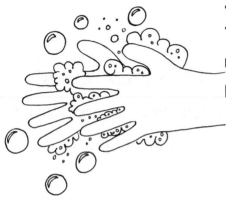

Step 4: Rinse the
soap off my hands
with water.

Step 5: Turn the water off.

Step 6: Dry my hands.

I will try to follow these steps when I wash my hands. Mom or Dad will help me practice these steps. I can learn to wash my hands.

Time to brush my teeth

People brush their teeth to keep them clean. Brushing my teeth helps to make a beautiful smile. Brushing my teeth helps to keep them healthy and strong. It is a smart idea to brush my teeth. Keeping my teeth clean is an intelligent thing to do.

When do people brush their teeth?

Many people brush their teeth two times each day. Usually people brush their teeth in the morning. Usually people brush their teeth before bed. I will try to brush my teeth two times a day. This is very intelligent. Brushing teeth is a healthy thing to do.

How do children learn to brush their teeth?

Adults teach children to brush their teeth. I am learning to brush my teeth. I will use my toothbrush. I will also use toothpaste and water. These are the steps:

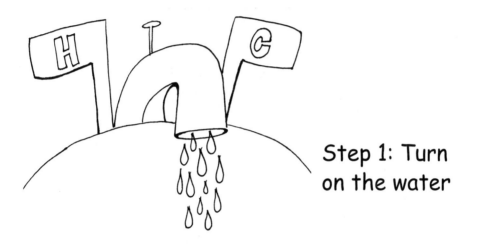

Step 1: Turn on the water

Step 2: Put water on the toothbrush

Step 3: Put a little toothpaste on the toothbrush

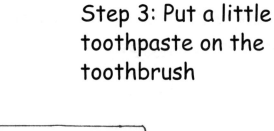

Step 4: Brush teeth by moving the toothbrush up and down

Step 5: Spit
toothpaste into
the sink

Step 6: Turn the
water off

I will try to follow these steps when I brush my
teeth. Mom or Dad will help me practice these
steps. I can learn how to brush my teeth.

Time to Take Medicine

Medicines help people. Some medicines help people who are ill. Some medicines help people think or feel better. Doctors decide if a person needs medicine.

Why is medicine special?

Very intelligent people make medicines in laboratories. Medicines come in many shapes, sizes, and forms. Sometimes medicine is in a bottle. Sometimes medicine is in another container. Directions are printed on the container. It is important for adults to follow these directions.

Why do adults give me medicine?

Adults may give me medicine to help my body. Sometimes I may be sick. Medicine can help me feel better. Adults may give me medicine for another reason. Taking medicine that adults give me is a smart thing to do.

When do adults give me medicine?

Doctors and other adults know when it is time for me to take my medicine. I may be given medicine in the morning. I may be given medicine at night. I may be given medicine at another time. It is important for me to take my medicine when an adult tells me.

What is liquid medicine?

Sometimes medicine is liquid. Liquid medicine comes in a bottle. Liquid medicine may be pink or blue or another color. Liquid medicines may taste like bubble gum, cherries, or other flavors. Moms and dads know how to give children liquid medicine. This will keep me safe.

What is a medicine spoon?

A medicine spoon measures my medicine. It has numbers on the side so Mom or Dad can measure my medicine. Moms and dads know how to pour the medicine in the spoon until it fills to the right number. I will try to drink my medicine carefully from the medicine spoon. That way, I will get the medicine that I need.

How do adults give me my medicine?

Adults give me my medicine. These are the steps:

1. The adult pours the medicine into my medicine spoon.

2. Sometimes the adult says, "Open wide!" That means please open my mouth.

3. The spoon goes into my mouth.

4. The medicine goes into my mouth.

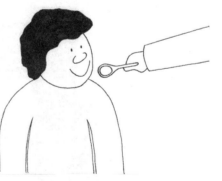

5. I will try to swallow the medicine.

Time to blow my nose

Snot is made in my nose. Sometimes when I get a cold my nose makes too much snot. Sometimes if I have an allergy my nose may make too much snot. Sometimes my nose makes too much snot for another reason. It's okay to blow or wipe away extra snot.

What does "blowing my nose" mean?

Sometimes my nose feels full. This means my nose has snot in it. People may say "your nose is stuffy." The air in my nose can push the snot out. This is called "blowing my nose."

What does "wiping my nose" mean?

Sometimes my nose is dripping. This means snot is dripping onto my face. People may say, "your nose is running." It may be time to wipe my nose. Wiping my nose means getting the snot off my face.

What do I use to blow or wipe my nose?

I use a tissue to blow or wipe my nose. A tissue is a soft cotton rectangle. Tissues come in many colors. They may be white. They may be another color. I may use tissues to blow or wipe my nose. Adults know where to find tissues.

How do I use a tissue?

Adults teach children to use a tissue. Adults may wipe or blow my nose for me. I may wipe or blow my nose myself. These are the steps:

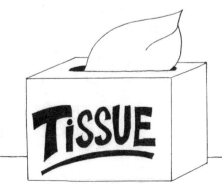

Step 1: Find a tissue box.

42

Step 2: Take a tissue out of the box.

Step 3: Put the tissue up to my nose.

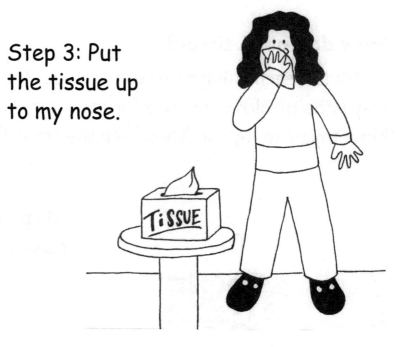

Step 4: Gently wipe or blow the snot into the tissue.

Step 5: Find a trashcan to put the used tissue

I will try to follow these steps when I wipe or blow my nose. An adult will help me practice these steps. That way I can learn to wipe or blow my nose myself.

Why do children need new clothes?

I wear clothes every day. I am growing a little bigger every day, too.

My clothes do not grow bigger. They may not fit me anymore.

Sometimes I get too big for my clothes. I have to get new ones.

My mom or dad may buy new clothes for me at the store. Sometimes other people give me clothes.

Bigger clothes fit better!

Why do I have new clothes?

I have new clothes. This is because my body is bigger and my other clothes are too small.

Where do children find new clothes?

Clothing stores have new clothes for children. They have clothes in many sizes. This makes it easy to find clothes that fit. Mom knows what clothes I need. Sometimes I know what clothes I want. We can shop to find new clothes.

How does it feel to wear new clothes?

Sometimes I wear new clothes for the first time. They may feel soft. They may feel a little stiff. Wearing clothes makes them older and softer. I will try to wear my new clothes.

When do I wear new clothes?

Mom or Dad know when it is time to wear new clothes. Sometimes I wear new clothes. Sometimes I wear old clothes. Sometimes I wear new clothes and old clothes at the same time. This is okay.

Choosing Clothes to Wear Outside

Sometimes it is cold outside. It is a good idea to wear clothes that keep me warm.

Sometimes it is warm outside. It is a good idea to wear clothes that keep me cool.

An adult knows which clothes will keep me comfortable.

What do people wear when it gets cold outside?

When it is cold outside people wear long sleeves and long pants. When it gets warm outside I need to wear warm weather clothes.

In warm weather people usually wear shirts with short sleeves and shorts. In warm weather wearing these clothes helps keep people cool and comfortable.

What do people wear when it gets warm outside?

When it is warm outside people can wear short sleeve shirts and short pants. When it gets cold outside I need to wear cold weather clothes.

People wear long sleeve shirts and long pants in cold weather. Having their arms and legs covered keeps people warm.

What is a coat?

Sometimes it is cold outside. A coat keeps me warm on a cold day. People wear coats when they are outside. Adults like it when I wear my coat to stay warm outside. Adults know coats help keep people warm. I will try to wear my coat when I am outside on cold days.

What is a mitten?

Sometimes it is cold outside. A mitten can keep my hand warm. A mitten is a little "coat" for my hand. Wearing two mittens keeps both hands warm. When it is cold outside I will try to wear mittens.

Sometimes my mittens may be attached to my coat. This keeps my mittens with me.

Why do people wear boots?

Sometimes people wear boots. People may wear boots when it is cold or wet weather. Boots may keep my feet warm. Boots may keep my feet dry. Sometimes it is intelligent to wear boots.

Time for a nap

A nap is sleeping for a short time during the day. Taking a nap is okay. I will try to take a nap. I may play later.

Why do I take naps?

Most young children take naps. Sometimes I take naps. A nap helps me to rest. Resting makes it easier to be awake. When I am awake I may do many things. Naps are good for me.

When is naptime?

Sometimes it is time to take a nap. Mom and Dad know when it is time to take a nap. They may know by looking at the clock. They may know by looking at me. They might know by talking with me. Mom or Dad will tell me when it's time to take a nap.

What do adults do when I am taking a nap at home?

When I take a nap at home, an adult stays near. The adult may read a book, wash clothes, or maybe do something else. An adult stays home when I sleep. An adult is nearby when I wake up.

How do children learn to take a nap?

Children learn to take naps with practice. I am learning to take a nap. These are the steps:

Step 1: Mom or Dad may read this story to me before naptime.

Step 2: Find a place to rest.

Step 3: Get comfortable and feel cozy.

Step 4: Think quiet thoughts. A sleeping kitten is a quiet thought. I might have quiet thoughts of my own.

Step 5: Close
my eyes.

Step 6: I may fall
asleep. I may just
think quiet thoughts
with my eyes closed.

Step 7: I will wake up or Mom or
Dad will tell me when naptime is
finished.

I will try to follow these steps when I take a
nap.

Time for a haircut

The hair on my head grows. Each day my hair grows a little longer. Sometimes it needs to be cut. An adult may say, "Time for a haircut." This means my hair needs to be shorter.

When do I get my haircut?

Mom and Dad know when my hair is too long. Mom and Dad know when hair needs to be cut. They may know by looking at the calendar. They may know by looking at me. Mom or Dad will take me to a hairstylist to get my hair cut.

What is a hairstylist?

A hairstylist is a man or woman who cuts hair. Hairstylists learn to cut hair at a special school. Hairstylists know how to cut hair.

The hairstylist uses a scissors or razor to cut hair. This makes hair shorter.

Where does a hairstylist work?

A hairstylist works in a shop. There are special chairs. These chairs go up and down safely. There are mirrors, too. People sit in the chairs. They look in the mirrors. They can watch the hairstylist cut their hair.

How can I help the hairstylist?

The hairstylist may say "Please sit still." I can help the hairstylist by sitting still. The hairstylist likes it when I try to sit still. Sitting still makes it easier for the hairstylist to cut my hair. Sometimes people talk while getting their haircut. They try to sit still and talk at the same time. It helps the hairstylist when people sit still.

What steps do I follow to get my haircut?

Hairstylists cut hair. Sometimes I get my hair cut by a hairstylist. I will try to follow these steps:

Step 1: Walk into the shop with Mom or Dad.

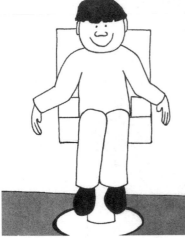

Step 2: Sit in the chair.

Step 3: The hairstylist will put on a cape. The cape keeps hair off of my clothing. It is a safe to wear the cape.

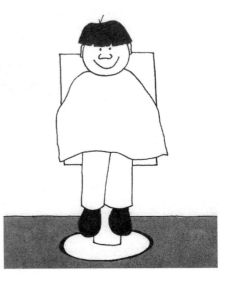

Step 4: Sit still
and listen for
directions.

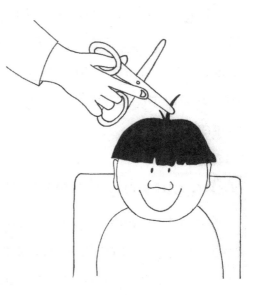

Step 5: Wait
for the
hairstylist to
cut my hair.

Step 6: The
hairstylist will take
the cape off of me.
This means my
haircut is finished.

Mom or Dad will help me learn these steps. I
can learn to help the hairstylist.

Time to clip my fingernails

Fingernails grow. When an adult says, "Let's clip your fingernails," they want to trim my fingernails a little shorter. They will clip the very tip of my fingernail. I will try to let an adult clip my fingernails.

Who cuts my fingernails?

An adult will clip my fingernails when they are too long. An adult knows how to use nail clippers to cut my fingernails. An adult knows how to safely clip my fingernails.

Is having my fingernails clipped safe?

It is safe for my fingernails to be clipped. An adult will be very careful when they clip my fingernails. An adult will try to make me feel safe when they clip my fingernails. Keeping my fingers still helps.

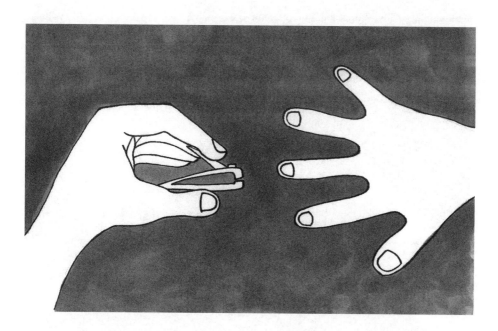

Time to clip my toenails

Toenails grow. When an adult says, "Lets clip your toenails," they want to trim my toenails a little shorter. They will clip the very tip of my toenail. I will try to let an adult clip my toenails.

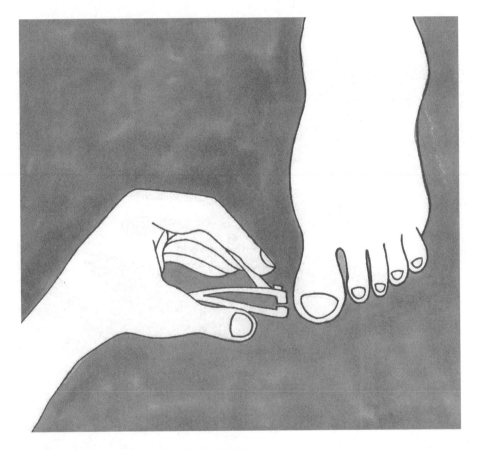

Who clips my toenails?

An adult will clip my toenails when they are too long. An adult knows how to use nail clippers to clip my toenails. An adult knows how to safely clip my toenails.

Is having my toenails clipped safe?

It is safe for my toenails to be clipped. An adult will be very careful when they clip my toenails. An adult will try to make me feel safe when they clip my toenails. Keeping my toes still helps.

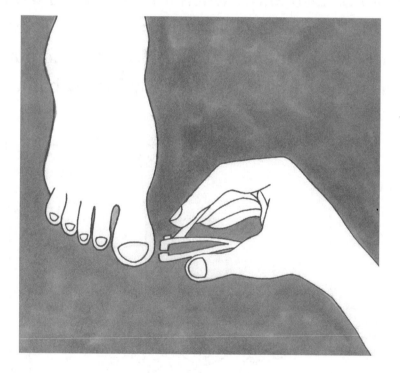

Time for a bath

Sometimes I get dirty. When I get dirty my parents want me to be clean. Most children take baths to get clean. I will try to take a bath when my parents tell me it's time to take one.

When do I take a bath?

Mom or Dad know when it is time for a bath. They might know by looking at the clock. They might know by looking at me. Mom or Dad put water in the bathtub to get ready for my bath.

Why do I leave my clothes outside the bathtub?

I try to take my clothes off before getting into the bathtub. This keeps my clothes dry. This makes it easier to wash my body. Leaving clothes outside the bathtub is an intelligent idea. It is an intelligent thing to do.

How do I get into the bathtub?

Mom or Dad help me get into the bathtub. This keeps me safe. Mom or Dad might take my hand to help me get into the bathtub. Mom or Dad might lift me into the bathtub. Mom or Dad will help me safely get into the bathtub.

How do adults help me take a bath?

Adults help children take a bath. Mom or Dad help me take a bath. These are the steps:

Step 1: Mom or Dad puts water in the bathtub.

Step 2:
Clothes off,
Mom or Dad
may help.

Step 3: Mom or
Dad help me get
into the
bathtub safely.

Step 4: Get
washed. Mom or
Dad may help.

Step 5: Sometimes
playing in the bathtub
is okay.

Step 6: Mom or Dad help me get out of the bathtub.

Step 7: Dry my body with a towel.

Step 8: Clothes on.

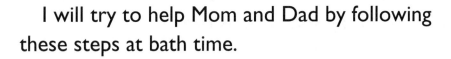

I will try to help Mom and Dad by following these steps at bath time.

Time to wash my hair

When I take a bath or shower I clean my body. Sometimes when I take a bath or shower I clean my hair too. This is called washing my hair. Washing my hair makes it clean and shiny. Washing hair is a smart thing to do.

What is shampoo?

Shampoo is special soap for hair. Sometimes shampoo is a liquid. When mixed with water, shampoo makes bubbles. The shampoo bubbles clean hair. Using shampoo is okay.

When does my hair get washed?

Sometimes my hair gets dirty and needs to be washed. Adults know when my hair is dirty. Adults know when it is time to wash my hair. An adult will tell me when it is time to wash my hair.

How do children learn to wash their hair?

Adults teach children to wash their hair. I am learning to wash my hair. These are the steps:

Step 1: Stand in the shower or in the bathtub. Put water on my hair.

Step 2: Put a little shampoo on my hand.

Step 3: Use the shampoo to make shampoo bubbles in my hair.

Step 4: Use water to
rinse the shampoo
bubbles away.

Use a towel to dry
my hair.

I will try to follow these steps when I wash my
hair. Mom or Dad will help me practice these
steps. I can learn to wash my hair.

What does it mean when people say, "Time to go to bed"?

All people sleep. Most people sleep on Monday, Tuesday, Wednesday, Thursday, Friday, Saturday, and Sunday nights. They wake up each morning.

I sleep in a bed. Usually Mom or Dad says, "Time to go to bed." This means it is time to get ready to get into bed and go to sleep.

When is bedtime?

Mom or Dad knows when it is my bedtime. They know by looking at the clock. Sometimes Mom or Dad knows it is my bedtime just by talking with me. When it is time to get ready to sleep Mom or Dad may say, "It's bedtime!" That means it is a good idea to go to bed and fall asleep.

Where do I sleep?

I have a bed. On my bed is my mattress. On my mattress are my sheets. Over my sheets is my blanket. At one end of my bed is my pillow. My pillow is for my head. It is okay to lie between my sheets, under my blanket, with my head on my pillow, and go to sleep. This is my bed and this is where I will try to sleep.

When do people go to bed?

Usually, children need to sleep longer than moms and dads. That is why I go to bed before my mom or dad. My bedtime is at about_____. My mom goes to bed at about_____. My dad goes to bed at about_____. It is okay for me to sleep when Mom and Dad are awake. They will go to bed soon. They have bedtime, too.

What is a dream?

Sometimes I dream while I sleep. A dream is like a video my mind makes all by itself. I can watch it with my eyes closed while I am asleep.

72

Sometimes a dream may be frightening. Then it is called a nightmare. Mom or Dad can help me if I have a nightmare. They can try to help me feel better.

How do I go to bed?

When Mom and Dad tell me it is bedtime, I can follow these steps to go to bed:

Step 1: Put on my pajamas.

Step 2: Get into bed.

Step 3: Try to close my eyes.

Step 4: Lay quietly until I am asleep.

Mom and Dad will help me learn these steps. Someday I may do these steps myself.

Chapter 2

Home

What are unexpected noises?

There are many noises. Sometimes noises surprise me. They are unexpected. Some unexpected noises are; telephones, doorbells, barking dogs, breaking glass, vacuum cleaners, slamming doors, honking horns, and thunder. These sounds are okay. I will try to stay calm when I hear unexpected noises. Adults can tell me when the noise will stop.

What is a telephone?

A telephone is an electronic device. Sometimes people use telephones to talk to people.

Sometimes people call on the telephone. I can hear the phone ring. This tells me someone is calling. The noise is unexpected.

When the phone is answered, the ringing will stop. Telephones are quiet most of the time.

What is a doorbell?

A doorbell is an electronic device. It is attached to a button by our door.

People push the button when they come to my home. It lets us know they are outside of our door. This makes a noise inside. The noise can be unexpected.

I will try to tell an adult when the doorbell rings. They will answer the door. Doorbells are quiet most of the time.

How do doors make noises?

Doors can make unexpected noises. Sometimes a door closes too fast. This is called a slamming door. A strong wind can slam a door shut. Sometimes people slam doors by pushing them too hard. The doors in my home are quiet most of the time.

Some doors make noises that are expected. When automatic doors open at the store, people know the door will make a noise.

Why do dogs bark?

Dogs bark for many reasons. Dogs may bark because they want to go outside or inside. Dogs may bark because someone is near their home. Dogs may bark at moving cars.

Barking is a noise that may be unexpected. Dogs are quiet most of the time.

What happens when people drop things?

When something drops to the floor, it may make a noise. It may be a loud noise. It may be a quiet noise. Things that are dropped make unexpected noises.

People drop all kinds of things. They try to hold on but accidentally let go. They drop glasses, pens, papers, books, plates, keys, and other things, too.

What is a vacuum cleaner?

A vacuum cleaner is an appliance that cleans. Mom and Dad know how to use a vacuum cleaner to clean a home. A vacuum cleaner has a switch. It turns the motor on. The motor makes a noise. A vacuum cleaner has a switch that turns the motor off. The noise stops.

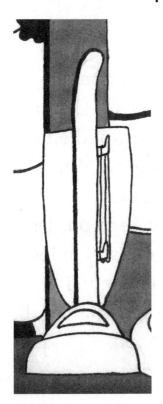

The motor of a vacuum moves air to pull away dirt and dust. Vacuum cleaners pull dirt away from carpets, draperies, and furniture. This helps people keep their homes clean. Vacuum cleaners are turned off most of the time.

Why do cars have horns?

Cars have horns to warn people of danger. This helps to keep people safe.

The horn is sometimes in the center of the steering wheel. When a driver pushes the horn it makes a very loud noise. Some drivers have a button on their key ring that starts the car horn.

People who are nearby do not expect to hear the horn. It surprises them and they look around. They may notice a dangerous situation in time to stop or get out of the way.

Car horns are quiet most of the time.

What is thunder?

Usually thunder is an unexpected noise. Thunder is the sound made by lightning. Lightning is a big electric spark in the sky. Most of the time, when there is thunder and lightning it is also raining. This is called a thunderstorm.

My mom and dad know how to keep our family very safe in a thunderstorm. We can stay indoors. Sometimes, we may watch the thunder and lightning through the window. If I see lightning, I can expect to hear thunder very soon.

The sky is quiet most of the time.

Who knows about time?

Sometimes it is time to play. Sometimes it is time to sleep. Sometimes it is time to eat. Sometimes it is time to work. Adults know when it is time to play, sleep, eat, and work. Adults know when it is time to do other things, too.

Who knows what time it is?

Adults know about time. Older children know about time, too.

They look at a clock to see what time it is.

They look at the clock to know if it is time to eat.

They look at the clock to know if it is time to play.

They look at the clock to know if it is time to work.

They look at the clock to know if it is time to sleep.

Knowing what time it is helps people know what to do.

What is a watch?

A watch is a very little clock that people wear on their wrist. A watch helps people know if it is time to eat, play, work, sleep, or do something else.

What does "hurry up" mean?

Sometimes people say, "Hurry up". If I am walking, "Hurry up" means "please walk faster". If I am putting on my coat, "Hurry up" means "please put the coat on faster". If I am putting my toys away, "Hurry up" means, "please put the toys away faster." Hurry up" means move faster. I will try to move faster when people say "Hurry up". It's important to them.

What does it mean to be "on time"?

Some things happen at certain times. Church and synagogue begin at the same time each week. School begins at the same time each school day. Birthday parties begin at a certain time, too. Arriving at the same time helps everyone begin activities together.

Sometimes people say they want to be "on time." That means they want to arrive and start when everyone else does. Sometimes people hurry up to be on time.

What does it mean to "be late"?

Sometimes people say they "do not want to be late". They are feeling nervous that something will start before they arrive. Sometimes people are late for church or synagogue. They may feel embarrassed when people watch them walk in late. Sometimes children are late for school. They may arrive after the teacher and the children start their day.

Most people think being on time is better than being late. That is why when they start to feel a little nervous about being late they hurry up.

Who is coming to play?

Sometimes children come to play at my home.
The child that is coming today is

_____.

_____is my friend today.

When will we play?

Today I am having a friend come to my home.
My friend will come at about _____.
My friend will leave at about _____. We can
play from _____ to _____.

What can I say when my friend arrives?

My friend is coming today at about _____.
When my friend arrives, I may say, "Hi!" Saying
"Hi" is a friendly thing to do. It helps my friend
feel welcome in my home.

What will we do today?

Today a friend is coming to my house. My mom
or dad can help us make a list of things we can do.
I may have some ideas about what we can do. My
friend may have some ideas too. A good list of
play ideas has my choices and my friend's choices,
too! This is called a Play Plan.

How do we use our Play Plan?

Our Play Plan is a list of things to do. My friend and I can look at the list. We can find something to do. Sometimes we may choose to do the same activity. It is okay to play alone for a while, too. My mom or dad can help us.

Do we always follow the Play Plan?

Sometimes my friend will have a new idea. I may have a new idea, too. If we hear the ice cream truck coming, we may decide to ask Mom or Dad if we can get an ice cream. If it is time for lunch, we may ask if we can help make lunch. We may see a book that we would like to have Mom or Dad read to us. We can decide to choose activities that are new ideas. They become part of our plan even if they are not added to our list.

Will my friend use my toys?

A friend is coming to my home. My friend knows I have toys. My friend is hoping to have a turn playing with my toys. I may let my friend play with my toys for a short time. This is called sharing my toys.

My friend knows my toys belong to me. He knows my toys stay with me when we are finished playing.

Someday, my friend may share his toys with me.

Who decides which toys we play with at my home?

Sometimes a friend comes to play at my home. Some of my toys are special to me. It is okay to put them away while my friend is over to play.

It is friendly to choose some of my toys to share with my friend. My mom or dad can help me choose good toys to share.

When it is time for my friend to leave, my shared toys stay with me.

What do I say when my friend leaves?

My friend is coming to my home today. We will play from _____ until about _____. When my friend has to leave, I might say, "Thank you for coming!" My friend may play at my home again. We may play at my friend's home sometime. Our parents can help us plan to play together.

How will we make plans to play again?

It will be easy for us to find my friend to make plans to play with my friend again. My parents have my friend's phone number. We can call to make plans to play. My parents have my friend's address. We know how to find my friend's home. We may even have my friend's e-mail address. There are many ways to ask my friend to play again.

What is taking turns?

Sometimes, children want to play with the same toy. They may need to take turns with the toy. A "turn" is a chance to play with the toy. Each child has a turn playing with the toy. This means that I will have a chance to play with the toy. I will have my turn with the toy.

When is it my turn?

Sometimes it may be difficult to know when it is my turn. Adults can help.

An adult may ask to me wait for my turn, saying, "_____, please wait." "Wait" means my turn is coming. "Wait" may also mean it's a good time to play with another toy. Adults will try to show me what "wait" means.

When it's my turn, someone may say, "_____, it's your turn!" That means other children will wait until my turn is finished.

Is it easy to take turns?

Sometimes children take turns easily. Sometimes it is more difficult. This is okay. It is usually easier for children to take turns when there is an adult to help them.

Sometimes children make mistakes when they are learning to take turns. Taking a toy from a child without asking is a mistake. An adult can help. Little by little, children learn what to do when someone makes a mistake taking turns.

Which toys are mine?

I have toys that are "my toys". These are the toys that stay with me in my home. My mom or dad may help me find a place to keep my toys.

My mom or dad may help me label my toys with a special sticker or my name. That will help me know for sure which toys are mine.

How can I get my toy back?

Once in a while, another child may take my toy while I am playing. I can say, "Please give my toy to me!" This may work.

Sometimes, the child may keep my toy after I ask for it back. I have a choice. I may ask the child again, "Please give my toy to me!" I may also choose to ask an adult for help. Adults know how to help children return toys.

Why do children make mistakes when they play?

Most children make mistakes once in a while when they play with others. They may accidentally break a toy. They may forget how to take turns. They may become tired and say something that is not very nice.

Making mistakes is how children learn to play together. Moms and dads can help when children make mistakes. They have ideas to help children have fun again.

How do children share a play area?

Sometimes children share one play area. Children need a little space when they play. A little space is about the length of my arm. Adults can help children learn to play with a little space around them. I can learn to play with a little space between me and the other children. A little space helps children feel comfortable and safe when they play.

How do children share video games?

People can learn to share video games. Sometimes it is my turn to play video games. Sometimes other people have a turn playing video games. I will try to let others have a turn playing video games. This is a friendly idea.

Can children share in cleaning up, too?

Sometimes toys have to be put away. Children learn to share in clean up. They work together at the same time. It takes a long time for one child to put all the toys away. It is faster if all of the children help to put the toys away. Putting toys away together makes cleaning up easier and faster.

What is a babysitter?

Sometimes I have a babysitter. A babysitter is a person who takes care of me when Mom and Dad are away.

The babysitter may come to my home to stay with me. The babysitter will leave when Mom and Dad return.

Sometimes I may stay at the babysitter's home. I will return to my home with Mom and Dad.

Why do I have a babysitter?

Sometimes I have a babysitter to take care of me when Mom and Dad are away.

My babysitter may make food for me.

My babysitter plays safely with me.

My babysitter may read me a story.

The babysitter leaves when Mom and Dad return.

What does my babysitter know about me?

Mom and Dad have told the babysitter about me. My babysitter knows how to take care of me. My babysitter knows when I play. My babysitter knows when I sleep. My babysitter knows what I like to do. My babysitter knows how to take care of me while Mom and Dad are away.

Where are Mom and Dad?

My babysitter takes care of me when my mom and Dad are away.

Sometimes I have a babysitter when my mom and dad are at work.

Sometimes I have a babysitter when my mom and dad are going to eat at a restaurant.

Sometimes I have a babysitter when my mom and dad go to a movie.

Sometimes Mom and Dad go other places, too. I can ask Mom or Dad where they are going. They will come back.

What is a new baby brother?

There is a new baby in our home. He is a very new person born a little while ago. He eats and sleeps and has a lot to learn. I can help. This baby is my new brother.

What is a new baby sister?

There is a new baby in our home. She is a very new person born a little while ago. She eats and sleeps and has a lot to learn. I can help. This baby is my new sister.

Who does Mom love?

I have a new baby in my home. Mom loves the new baby. Mom loves me, too. Mom has plenty of love for all of her children.

Who does Dad love?

I have a new baby in my home. Dad loves the new baby. Dad loves me, too. Dad has plenty of love for all of his children.

When will the baby talk?

Someday the baby will learn to talk. It will take about a year for our baby to learn to use words. Most babies start to talk after their first birthday. Until then, the baby will cry once in a while. Adults know what to do when a baby cries.

Why do babies cry?

Babies cry for many reasons. Most of the time, babies cry when they are hungry. Babies may cry when they have a dirty diaper. Babies may cry when they are sick. Babies cry for other reasons, too. Crying is how babies let others know they need help.

Why do babies laugh?

Babies learn to laugh. It takes a few months for a baby to learn to laugh. Babies laugh for many reasons. Usually, babies laugh when they are happy and comfortable.

How can I help with the baby?

Mom and Dad know how to help our new baby. Mom or Dad knows what to do when the baby cries. Mom or Dad knows what to do when the baby needs help.

I can help our new baby, too. Mom or Dad can show me how I can help. A baby likes to have a helpful brother or sister. I will try to stay calm and learn how to help.

What does divorce mean?

Sometimes a mom and dad will divorce. A divorce means they have decided to live apart.

My parents were married. Now they are divorced.

Parents who are divorced love their children very much. Mom loves me a lot. Dad loves me a lot.

Why do some parents live in separate homes?

Each child has two parents.

Some children have parents who live in the same home. These parents are married.

Some children have parents who live in separate homes. These parents are divorced.

Mom lives in one home. Dad lives in another home. Mom and Dad are divorced.

What does it mean when Mom says, "We are going to Dad's home?"

Mom says I am going to Dad's home. That means I will visit my dad. That also means I may go to other places. My dad and I may go out to eat. My dad and I may go to other places. Going to Dad's home may mean going to other places, too. This is okay.

What does it mean when Dad says, "We are going to Mom's home?"

Dad says I am going to my mom's home. That means I will visit my mom. That also means I may go other places. My mom and I may go out to eat. My mom and I may go to other places. Going to Mom's home may mean going to other places. This is okay.

Why do I have a step-dad?

Many children have a step-dad. I have a step-dad. First, my mom and dad divorced. Then my mom married my step-dad. My mom and step-dad live in the same home.

Why do I have a step-mom?

Many children have a step-mom. I have a step-mom. First, my mom and dad divorced. Then my dad married my step-mom. My dad and my step-mom live in the same home.

Chapter 3

Going Places

Why do adults "forget"?

Sometimes adults have many things to do. They may have many things to think about. Sometimes they forget. My dad may forget to stop and buy milk. He should be thinking about getting milk, but he is thinking about something else. He may drive past the store where we buy milk. This is okay. Moms and dads forget other things, too.

What happens when Mom and Dad remember?

People usually remember what they forget. When this happens, they might say, "Oh-oh, I forgot!" When my dad remembers the milk, he might say, "Oh-oh, I forgot the milk!" This means he remembers that we need to buy milk. He may decide to turn around and go to buy the milk. I will try to stay calm when adults forget and then remember.

Why do people make lists?

People make lists. A list helps people remember. Sometimes people make lists of places they need to go. Sometimes people make lists of items they need to buy.

What does it mean to "run a few errands"?

Sometimes we have a few errands to run,
This means we have places to go,
We may do our errands and also have fun,
We'll return in an hour or so.

What do people do at a car wash?

Sometimes we go to the car wash to clean their car, van, or truck.

Sometimes people stay in the car. They ride safely in the car through the car wash. This is okay.

Sometimes people get out of their car. The car goes through the car wash without them. This is okay, too!

Adults know what to do at the car wash. They can help me learn what to do at the car wash, too!

What happens at a gas station?

My family has a car. Our car has a motor. The motor needs gas to work. The car uses gas to move.

A gas station is a gas store. We go to the gas station to buy gas for our car. Mom and Dad know how to put gas into the car. We pay for our gas. Gas keeps our car going.

Why are we going to the bank?

People need places to keep their money. There are many kinds of banks. I keep my money in a bank at home.

Mom and Dad keep a lot of their money in a very big bank. It is a building. Sometimes they visit the bank to put their money in. Sometimes they visit the bank to take their money out. Usually, people visit a bank for a very short time.

Children can help by waiting quietly while their parents visit the bank.

Why do people visit libraries?

A library has books for people to share. People can read the books in the library. Sometimes, people borrow the books. They sign the books out and take them home. People return books to the library when they are finished reading them.

Each person in the library tries to talk and move quietly. This helps the people who are reading. I will try to talk quietly when we visit the library

Where are we going?

Sometimes we go places. I have a book about going places. My book has photographs of places I go. Sometimes I go shopping. Sometimes I go to visit someone. Sometimes I go to school. Sometimes I go to another place. It's okay to go places.

Sometimes I may go to a place that is not in my going places book. This is okay. We may take a photo when we get there. I may add the photograph to my book about going places!

When will we leave?

Adults and older children know about time.

They look at the clock. They can tell it is almost time to go. They may say, "It's time to get ready to go!"

They look at the clock again. They can tell it is time to go. They may say, "It's time to go!" That means it is time to leave.

Knowing what time it is helps people know what to do next.

Who knows the way?

I ride in the car to go to many places. I may ride in the car to go to school or the store. I may ride in the car to other places, too. Usually, Mom or Dad will drive.

Mom or Dad usually drives on the same roads when we visit these places. Sometimes Mom or Dad may use other roads to drive to these places. They know another way to get there.

It's okay to take other roads to travel to the school, the store, or other places.

When will we get there?

Sometimes children ride in a car. They are going some place. They may ask their mom or dad, "When will we get there?" That's because children want to know how long they will be sitting in the car.

Adults can make a guess about how long it will take to get there. Mom may say, "I think we will be there in about ten minutes." She is trying to make a very good guess.

Why are we still in the car?

Sometimes there are many cars on the road. This is called "a lot of traffic." When there is a lot of traffic it may take a little longer to get where we are going.

Mom may say, "Oh, I didn't expect all this traffic!" This means she is surprised. She thought there would be fewer cars on the road.

Mom has learned something new. Now she can make a better guess about when we will get there. This time she may be right.

What is a grocery store?

A grocery store has apples and tea,
All kinds of food for my family – and
me!
A grocery store has milk, eggs, and
bread…
Of course, my family may buy other
food instead,
It's a store with groceries, that's what
it's for,
That's why they call it a grocery store!

What will we buy at the grocery store?

Sometimes we go to the grocery store. My
mom or dad may go with me. My mom or dad
may go alone or with someone else. They know
what food we need. They know what food we can
leave on the shelf at the store. This is important.

May I have this?

Sometimes I go to the grocery store. If I want something off the shelf, I will try to ask first. I may ask, "May I have this?" Asking is the first step. Waiting for the answer is the second step. Sometimes the answer is "yes". Sometimes the answer is "no". This is okay.

What is a check out?

I am going to the grocery store. Before we leave the store, we will go to the check out.

The check out is an important step in grocery shopping. This is where we give the cashier money. The money pays for the food. The check out is also where our food is placed in bags.

Why do we wait in check out lines?

It's very important for people to pay for their food at the grocery store. They may need to stand in a checkout line.

Some people may be ahead of us in line. They will pay for their food. Then we will pay for our food.

Some people may be behind us in line. We will pay for our food first. Then the people behind us will pay for their food.

Standing in the check out line helps people take turns paying for their food.

Why do we always pick the slowest line?

Sometimes my mom or dad may say, "I always pick the slowest line." They really didn't know it was the slowest line when they chose it. They tried to choose the line that would get them out of the store quickly. When Mom or Dad says, "I always pick the slowest line," what they mean is that it feels like they always end up in a line where they have to wait for a long time. They are feeling a little frustrated and unlucky.

Can I help?

I may be helpful at the grocery store. How many ways? At least 5, maybe more:

1. It helps if I sit still in the cart while I ride.

2. It helps if I talk quietly inside the grocery store.

3. It helps if I look for the items we need.

4. It helps if I listen when adults talk to me.

5. It helps if I hold the cereal or bread.

6. It's okay if I hold something else instead.

Being helpful may make shopping more fun. If everyone helps, then the shopping gets done!

What do people do at the beach?

Sometimes people say, "Let's go to the beach!" The beach is a sandy place near water. People like to do many things at the beach.

Some people may go to the beach to swim in the water. It's important to swim with an adult.

Some people may go to the beach to sit on the sand.

Some people may go to the beach to lie down to enjoy the warm sun.

Some people may go to the beach to build sandcastles.

Many people like to visit the beach. I may like it too!

What will I do at the video store?

A video store is a place where people go to rent movies. There are many movies and games in the video store.

Mom or Dad will help me choose a movie to rent. Some movies are for children. Some movies are for adults. Moms and dads know which movies are for children.

I may help to choose a movie or game at the video store!

What is a zoo?

The zoo is a place with many animals. The animals live at the zoo. A zoo may have monkeys, lions, tigers, and other animals, too! People called zookeepers take care of the animals.

When we visit the zoo, Mom or Dad will walk with me to see the animals. We may be able to ride on a small train.

Sometimes the animals will be awake. Sometimes the animals will be sleeping.

Many people like to visit the animals at the zoo!

What is a movie theatre?

A movie theatre has many seats and a large screen. That way many people can watch one movie at the same time.

Sometimes we go to the movie theatre. My mom or dad may hold my hand while we wait to buy our ticket. Other people will be buying tickets, too.

Sometimes I eat popcorn or a snack at the movie.

Sometimes I may get something to drink.

I will try to sit quietly in the theater. I will try to watch the movie.

Visiting the movie theater may be fun!

What does it mean to "eat out"?

Sometimes someone says, "Let's eat out."
"Let's eat out" means, "Let's eat at a restaurant."
A restaurant is one place where many people may
eat at the same time. McDonalds and Burger King
are restaurants. There are many other
restaurants, too.

Where will we eat?

There are many restaurants where people can
eat. Sometimes, my family has to choose one
restaurant. We may eat at McDonalds. We may

eat at Burger King. We may eat at another restaurant.

Who decides where we will eat?

Sometimes Mom chooses where we eat. This is ok.

Sometimes Dad chooses where we eat. This is ok.

Sometimes I can choose where we eat. This is ok, too!

Sometimes Mom or Dad says, "Where will we go to eat?"

We try to talk about it and choose a restaurant together.

How will we get to the restaurant?

Mom or Dad knows how to find the restaurant. They know the directions to the restaurant.

They know the best way to travel to the restaurant, too. Sometimes, it is best to ride in our car to the restaurant. Sometimes, it is best to ride in a bus or taxi. Sometimes, we can walk to the restaurant.

Who knows how to find the restaurant and the best way to travel there? Mom or Dad knows!

What is a booster seat?

Sometimes people sit at tables. Big people sit on chairs. They reach the table easily.

Sometimes, small people sit on booster seats. Sitting on a booster seat helps small people reach the table, too!

I am a small person. A booster seat may help me sit at a big table. Chairs and booster seats help people of different sizes sit at the same table.

What can I do while I wait for my food?

Sometimes people who visit restaurants have to wait. It's okay for children to draw, read, color, or play with a favorite toy to make waiting easier. If we have to wait, I can try to play quietly. Waiting quietly will help me and my mom or dad!

What is a menu?

A menu is a list of all the food choices in a restaurant. Some restaurants serve peanut butter and jelly. Some restaurants do not. Some restaurants serve macaroni and cheese. Some restaurants do not. Some restaurants have fish. Others have hamburgers, hot dogs, or fries. The menu helps people know what food choices they have.

What does it mean to "run out"?

Sometimes a restaurant may
"run out" of chicken,
Sometimes a restaurant may
"run out" of fries,
Sometimes a restaurant may
"run out" of applesauce,
What does it mean to "run out"
of supplies?
It means that they had it,
and now it is gone,
They are sorry and may have it later,
If they could get it,
they'd serve it right now,
"Can you choose something else?"
says the waiter.
There's always a choice
when the first one is gone,
There is choice number two or three,
My mom or dad may help me decide,
What food we can order for me!

When do I use the spoon and fork?

There are many kinds of food. Some food we eat with our hands. Some food we eat with a spoon or a fork. Adults help children learn when to use a spoon or a fork. I will try to use a spoon or a fork when adults ask me to.

How do restaurants make so much food?

Every restaurant has a kitchen. The kitchen has big stoves, ovens, sinks, and counters to make the food. (In our kitchen at home we have a stove, oven, a sink, and a counter, too!) The kitchen at a restaurant is very busy. The cook works in the kitchen of a restaurant.

Who is the cook?

A cook works in a restaurant kitchen. Sometimes, cooks wear white jackets and tall white hats. Sometimes, they wear something else. A cook has learned how to cook food for many people. The cook knows how to cook many kinds of food. The cook makes the food and gives it to the waiter or waitress.

What is a waiter?

The waiter is a man. He asks the people in the restaurant what they would like to eat. Then, he tells the cook. The cook makes our food. The waiter brings our food to us.

What is a waitress?

A waitress is a woman. She asks the people in the restaurant what they would like to eat. Then, she tells the cook. The cook makes our food. The waitress brings our food to us.

Who washes the dishes?

With so many people eating, there are many plates that need to be washed. Some moms and dads think that the best part about eating out is that someone else washes the dishes. The dishwasher in a restaurant washes all the dishes. This makes the dishes clean so they can be used again.

When will my school bus come?

Usually, I ride on a bus to my school. My school bus comes at about the same time each school day. Mom or Dad knows the days that I ride the school bus. They know when the bus is coming. They know when I need to be ready to go. It is helpful when I am dressed and ready when the bus arrives.

What do bus drivers know?

The person who drives my bus is the bus driver. My bus driver knows how to drive to my school. My bus driver knows how to keep children safe.

How can I help my bus driver?

I can help as we ride to school,
I can try to follow each rule,
Rule number 1: Sit quietly in my seat
and stay,
Rule number 2: Stand up when the
driver says it's okay.
It's smart to follow rules number
1 and 2,
Keeping me safe and others, too!

What is a school?

A school is a place where I learn with other children. Children learn while they work and play. A teacher helps the children learn.

My school will have puzzles and toys. My school will have tables and chairs. My school will have markers and paper. My school will have other things, too. My school will have a picture schedule, too!

What does a teacher know?

My teacher knows all about children – like me!
My teacher knows how to lead,
My teacher knows all about "what comes
    next..."
My teacher knows how to read.
My teacher knows all about colors and shapes,
My teacher knows numbers, too.
It's important to listen when my teacher talks,
Because my teacher knows what we will do!

What will I do at school?

My school has a picture schedule. The picture schedule shows us what to do. My teacher has a picture for group time. My teacher has a picture for snack time, too. My teacher has pictures for other activities, too. We try to follow the pictures. That way, we have time for each activity!

What is a doctor?

A doctor is a person who knows a lot about keeping healthy. A doctor can help someone who is sick. Doctors work very hard to keep people healthy.

What is a check-up?

Sometimes I may visit the doctor for a check-up. The doctor may ask me to step on a scale, stand tall, or open my mouth. The doctor may look in my ears, too. The doctor may ask me questions, or do other things, too. This is how a doctor checks to make sure I am healthy.

Sometimes the doctor may prescribe other tests. Tests can help my doctor learn about me. It's okay to have medical tests as part of a check-up.

Who can help me when I am sick?

Sometimes I may have a stuffy nose. Sometimes I may sneeze a lot, cough a lot, or my throat may hurt. Sometimes my stomach may hurt. I may be sick. Mom and Dad can help.

Sometimes when I am sick a doctor can help. The doctor will tell Mom and Dad how to help me feel better. Mom and Dad may give me medicine. The doctor knows how to help me feel healthy again.

Where do doctors work?

Doctors work in doctor's offices and hospitals. There is a reason for this. This makes it easier for doctors. Doctor's offices and hospitals have tongue depressors, stethoscopes, tables with paper, charts with pictures of hearts and ears, machines, and many other things that doctors need to help people stay healthy. If a doctor had to carry all of those things around, the doctor would soon be very tired. Children help their doctors by visiting them at doctors' offices or at the hospital.